THE SECRET WORLD OF

Kangaroos

THE SECRET WORLD OF

Kangaroos

Malcolm Penny

RAINTREE
STECK-VAUGHN
PUBLISHERS

A Harcourt Company

Published by Raintree Steck-Vaughn Publishers, an imprint of Steck-Vaughn Company

Acknowledgments
Project Editors: Sean Dolan and Rebecca Hunter
Production Manager: Richard Johnson
Illustrated by Robert Morton
Designed by Ian Winton

Planned and produced by Discovery Books

Library of Congress Cataloging-in-Publication Data
Penny, Malcolm
Kangaroos / Malcolm Penny.
p. cm. -- (Secret world of--)
Includes bibliographical references (p.).
ISBN 0-7398-4986-7

Printed and bound in the United States

1 2 3 4 5 6 7 8 0 LB 05 04 03 02

Contents

CHAPTER 1
The Big Four

The eastern gray kangaroo, which lives mainly in wooded country, is commonly called the "forester."

The western gray is sometimes called the "stinker" because the males give off a strong odor.

Female red kangaroos are usually gray-blue rather than red. Australians call them "blue fliers" because they can hop so fast.

Reds are the most numerous type of kangaroo, with a population of more than 8 million.

The most unusual type of wallaroo lives on Barrow Island, which was cut off from the Australian mainland about 13,000 years ago.

Bounding across the endless open plains of the Australian outback, a red kangaroo is unmistakable, a sight seen nowhere else on Earth but recognized by almost everyone in the world. The red, however, is just one of four kinds, or species, of kangaroo.

Kangaroos belong to a very special group of mammals called marsupials. Like all mammals, kangaroo mothers feed their young on milk before they can eat solid food; but marsupial babies are tiny and only half-developed when they are born. They complete their development while attached to a teat inside a pouch on their mother's belly. When grown, kangaroos are unique both in the way they look and in the way they move—they are the only large mammals that move by hopping on their hind legs.

Some marsupials, such as the opossum, remain native to the Americas. Today, however, most of the world's species of marsupials are found in Australia and New Guinea.

Tail
Long, heavy tail for balance at speed, support when moving slowly.

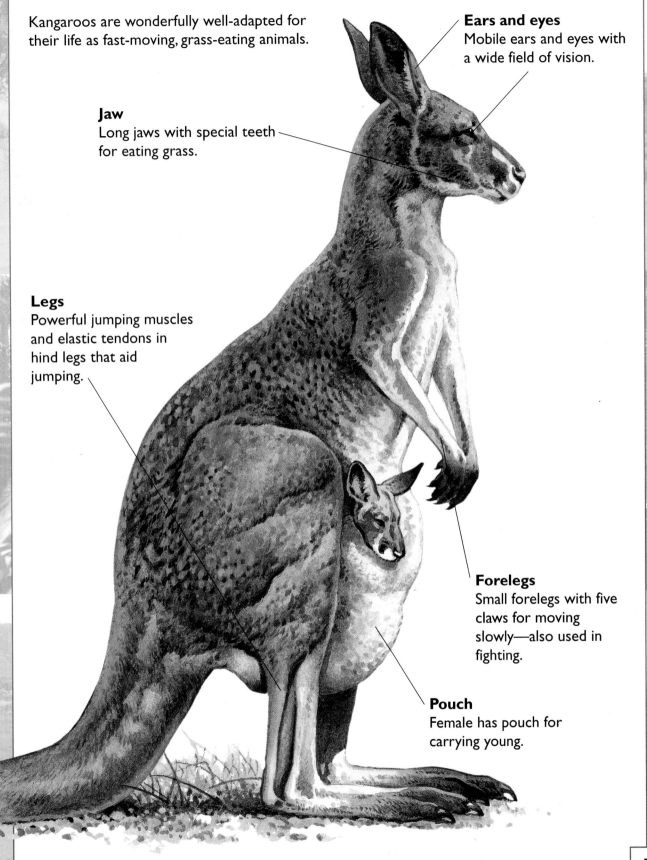

Kangaroos are wonderfully well-adapted for their life as fast-moving, grass-eating animals.

Ears and eyes
Mobile ears and eyes with a wide field of vision.

Jaw
Long jaws with special teeth for eating grass.

Legs
Powerful jumping muscles and elastic tendons in hind legs that aid jumping.

Forelegs
Small forelegs with five claws for moving slowly—also used in fighting.

Pouch
Female has pouch for carrying young.

EARLY MARSUPIALS

The first marsupials were small, tree-living animals somewhat like today's opossums. They first appeared about 75 million years ago, in North America. By about 23 million years ago, marsupials had spread through South America and across Antarctica—which was warm at the time—to the single vast land mass that was to become Australia and New Guinea.

I DIDN'T KNOW THAT

The Wonderful "Kanguroo"

The first kangaroos to be seen by Europeans were at Endeavour Bay, near what is now Cooktown in Queensland, Australia, where the explorer James Cook's ship was beached for repairs after being wrecked on the Great Barrier Reef in 1770. The scientists on the expedition asked the inhabitants of the place (Australia's native peoples are referred to as Aborigines) what these strange creatures were called. Their reply, which sounded like "kang-u-roo," became the first Aboriginal word to be used in the English language.

THE WONDERFUL
KANGUROO
FROM
BOTANY BAY

This land mass would soon split off from South America and Antarctica, allowing marsupials like the kangaroo and koala to evolve without competition from the placental mammals, such as dogs and hoofed animals, that evolved in other parts of the world.

There are two groups of marsupials loosely referred to as "kangaroos"—the macropodids ("big feet") and the potoroids. The macropodid family includes tree kangaroos, hare wallabies, nailtail wallabies, and rock, forest, and scrub wallabies—and the genus Macropus, the true kangaroos. Potoroids are smaller animals, many of which are called rat-kangaroos.

TRUE KANGAROOS

This book will focus on the four largest species of true kangaroo. The biggest is the red kangaroo of the open plains, which stands over 5 feet (1.6 m) tall, and can weigh more than 190 pounds (90 kg). Next in size are the two gray kangaroos, the eastern gray, or forester, and the western gray, or mallee, kangaroo. These make their homes in woodlands and thick brush. They are only slightly shorter than the red kangaroo, and weigh in at around 154 pounds (70 kg). The fourth type of true kangaroo, is the antilopine kangaroo, or wallaroo, sometimes called the euro or hill kangaroo, which lives in the tropical north of Australia and weighs about 121 pounds (55 kg).

Smaller Macropus species include the whiptail or prettyface wallaby, often called the flier, and the Tammar and Parma wallabies. They all weigh about 110 pounds (50 kg).

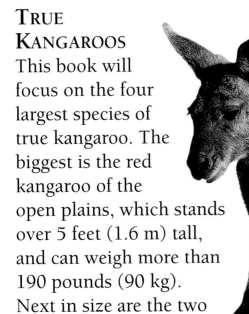

A wallaroo in northern Australia shows the unmistakable outline of a true kangaroo, with powerful tail and hind legs, and small forelegs, like arms.

CHAPTER 2
Little Big Feet

All kangaroos are vegetarians, except rat-kangaroos, which sometimes eat baby birds as well as insects.

The burrowing bettong is the only kangaroo that lives underground.

Long-nosed potoroos have been extinct in Western Australia since 1908, though they are still quite common in Tasmania.

The largest potoroid is the red-necked wallaby, which can be 35 inches (90 cm) tall and weigh 55 pounds (25 kg).

Only the musky rat-kangaroo regularly gives birth to twins.

WALLABIES

Different species of kangaroo are adapted to different habitats, but all are similar in build. Among the smaller macropodids, hare wallabies earned their English name because of their long ears and their way of bounding about in grasslands and low scrub, which reminded the English and Irish settlers of Australia of hares (rabbits) back home.

The spectacled hare wallaby of Barrow Island, off Western Australia, never drinks water, even

Although the spectacled hare wallaby of mainland Australia is the only species still considered to be common over the northern half of the continent, its habitat is threatened by grass-burning.

The red-necked pademelon is a forest kangaroo, living in damp woodland in eastern New South Wales and Queensland.

on the rare occasions when it rains on its arid island home. It obtains all the water it needs from the plants it eats.

Nailtail wallabies are small grassland animals that are preyed on by dogs and foxes. One species, the crescent nailtail wallaby, is already extinct; another, the bridled nailtail, is endangered.

The pademelons, or scrub wallabies, live, as their name suggests, in the dense, low bush that once covered much of southern Australia. As agriculture spread and the scrub was cleared to make way for farmland, their habitat has dwindled. Some species are now very rare.

THE QUOKKA

A little short-tailed wallaby, the quokka, is a tourist attraction on Rottnest Island, near Perth, Western Australia. Once it was very common all along the damp southwestern coast, but after foxes were introduced in 1920 it quickly became scarce. It survives in large numbers only on islands where no predators live. It gave Rottnest Island its name: a Dutch sea-captain in the late 17th century thought that the swarms of quokkas were rats. ("Rottnest" means "rats' nest" in Dutch.) Today, the "rats" charm visitors to the island by their tameness. They have no fear of people and line up to be fed tidbits and slices of bread.

The quokka weighs only 7 pounds (3.25 kg) and has a very short tail. Perhaps it is easy to see how a Dutch explorer mistook it for a rat.

TREE KANGAROOS

Tree kangaroos are the least kangaroo-like of the whole macropodid family. Their hind legs are relatively short—though they can hop like other kangaroos when they come down to the ground—and their forelegs are much thicker and stronger than those of other kangaroo species. They have wide hind feet with which they walk up and down tree

The sturdy build and thick forelegs of a tree kangaroo are adapted for climbing. This one was photographed in the forests of Papua New Guinea.

trunks, using the strong claws on their forefeet to cling with. Tree kangaroos are the only kangaroos that can move their hind legs independently; all the others move both legs together, except when they are swimming.

POTOROIDS

Of the 57 species of kangaroo, more than half are potoroids. Perhaps the most unusual of these are the rat-kangaroos: small, round-eared omnivores that feed by night in dense cover on the forest floor. They have their own unique way of gathering nesting material. They collect grasses and ferns in their mouths and drop the bundle on the ground. Then they kick it backward with their hind feet and gather it up in their prehensile tail to carry it to the nest.

THE MUSKY RAT-KANGAROO

The musky rat-kangaroo, named for the scent it produces from a gland under its tail, may be

The missing link? A musky rat-kangaroo on the forest floor in Queensland may be the nearest resemblance to the tree-living ancestors of modern kangaroos.

the "missing link" to the extinct ancient marsupials that lived in trees. About the size of a rat, it has several features that are no longer seen in "modern" kangaroos. For example, it still has movable first toes on its hind feet, something that all other members of the group have lost, though like all kangaroos, it has a special grooming claw that it uses to comb its fur. Also, instead of hopping, it gallops across the ground on all fours. When it is walking slowly, it holds its tail up in the air. Unlike the other rat-kangaroos, it is active by day.

POTOROOS AND BETTONGS

Potoroos, which give their name to the family, range in size from 13 to 16 inches (34 to 41 cm) with a tail about the same length, and weigh about 2 to 4.5 pounds (1-2 kg). They are mousy-colored animals, with pointed noses similar to those of rats. Like rat-kangaroos, they live in woodland undergrowth, where they feed on roots and stems.

The other small potoroids are the bettongs that live in dry eucalyptus forests wherever there is dense ground cover. They can weigh up to 7.5 pounds (3.5 kg). Nocturnal, they spend the day in one of several nests.

Without Water!

The brush-tailed bettong, which lives in the open forests of southwest Australia, can manage without liquid water, getting all the moisture it needs from bulbs and underground fungi. In 1859, St. Francis Island in South Australia was said to be "swarming" with brush-tailed bettongs. Cats were introduced to hunt them, and by the early 20th century, they were all gone.

I DIDN'T KNOW THAT

CHAPTER 3
Why So Timid and So Fast?

As used by the Aborigines, heavy hunting boomerangs, or wooden throwing clubs called waddies, can bring down a kangaroo at a distance of 160 feet (50 m).

The remains of ancient pitfall traps dug by Aborigines to catch kangaroos can still be found in parts of the outback.

Kangaroos need less than one-third of the water required by sheep. Red kangaroos can go without water for up to 12 days, even in hot weather.

Aborigines used every part of a kangaroo, using the bones to make tools and the sinews as string.

The marsupial lion was a predator of ancient kangaroos. It became extinct about 30,000 years ago, after the first people arrived in Australia.

There is no doubt that kangaroos, even the biggest of them, are prey animals, which might seem strange since there are no large native predators in Australia today. Their nervous behavior, big, watchful eyes, and mobile, alert ears

The big, watchful eyes and large ears of an eastern gray kangaroo suggest that it was a prey animal some time in the past.

Red kangaroos can bound effortlessly over the open plains for hours on end.

indicate that they were hunted at some time in their evolutionary past. Their speed when they are disturbed is further evidence that they have evolved to run for their lives. They behave like startled deer or alarmed antelope. Why should this be?

PREDATORS

The Tasmanian wolf, or thylacine, was hunted to extinction in the wild, and the last known specimen died in Hobart Zoo in 1936. The largest marsupial carnivore known today is the Tasmanian devil, which is only about 2 feet (60 cm) long. It is much too small to hunt large kangaroos. Why, then, are all kangaroos so timid, ready to flee at the slightest disturbance?

CARNIVOROUS KANGAROOS

One clue comes from discovery of the fossil bones of large carnivorous kangaroos, which probably hunted smaller kangaroos. The last of these died out between 1 and 2 million years ago. Modern kangaroos should have lost their fear of predators since then. But there is another factor that might have kept them hopping—the arrival of the first humans in Australia.

EARLY KANGAROOS

People first crossed into Australia from the north, through what is now New Guinea. No one is sure exactly when they arrived, but it might have been as long ago as 60,000 years. Archaeological evidence shows that Aborigines lived around the Murray River in southeastern Australia 40,000 years ago. They must have found their new homeland to be extraordinary—filled as it was with giant animals, moving in a way they had never seen before. Early on, they surely must have learned to hunt and kill these animals. Scientists know much about these early kangaroos from their fossilized remains.

A western gray—looking much browner than the eastern—stands ready to dart for cover in the eucalyptus forests where it lives.

FOSSIL EVIDENCE

The teeth of some fossil kangaroos show that they were browsers, not grazers—that is, they ate leaves from trees rather than grazing on grass. They would have needed a large stomach to digest this tough, rather indigestible food. For this reason, they must have been heavy, somewhat slow-moving animals, unlike the slim, bounding kangaroos of today. These fossil giants are known as the sthenurine kangaroos, as opposed to the macropodines, which are the ancestors of today's macropodids.

An archaeological dig in New South Wales (a state in Australia) was found to contain the bones of sthenurines alongside Aboriginal stone tools, proving that people lived in Australia while the giant browsing kangaroos were still alive. Indeed, it now seems certain that hunting by humans was what drove them to extinction.

The sthenurines had stout legs, with long thighs but rather short shins. This indicates that they could hop very fast, but only with short strides and probably only for short distances, perhaps as they darted for cover. This would have protected them against the carnivorous giants of the old days, but it was no defense against the persistent, organized hunting bands of the Aborigines. These ancient hunters wiped out all the many different species of sthenurines, even the small ones, before they turned their attention to the swift macropodines, which were much harder to catch. Their descendants have survived, nervously, to this day using their speed to avoid danger.

Kangaroo Rock Art

Aborigines made paintings in caves or on rock faces in specially selected places with religious or historic significance to the local people. Although some of the

paintings are centuries old, many are still restored every year by members of the local family that has inherited the responsibility. When the last of that family dies, the paintings are no longer restored, though they are still treated with reverence by the local peoples.

I DIDN'T KNOW THAT

CHAPTER 4
High-Speed Hopping

Although they live in a mainly dry climate, kangaroos are good swimmers, using their hind legs separately in a kind of "dog paddle."

Only tree kangaroos can move their hind legs separately out of water.

At full speed, a red kangaroo's leaps may be more than 20 feet (6 m) long.

The bouncing movement during hopping pumps air in and out of the kangaroo's lungs, saving it the energy needed to breathe.

The thing about kangaroo[s] most astonished the first Europeans to see them is they can hop at high spee[d] back legs, for long distan[ce] only other mammals that this way are small desert and some of the tree-dwe[llers] lemurs of Madagascar, wh[ich] are forced to come to the

When humans try it, hopping seems an inefficient way to move. The effort used in bouncing up and down on both feet produces only slow forward movement— unless we dive ahead, in which case we cannot move our feet forward quickly enough to save us from falling on our face. We can move more quickly by leaning our body

Perfectly balanced and superbly equipped, a red kangaroo at full speed is a magnificent sight. The heavy tail acts as a counter balance each time it lands.

forward, but only if we move one leg forward at a time to keep us from falling over. We call this "running."

Kangaroos "run" with both back feet at once—a method of movement that for them is both fast and efficient. Since four-legged animals (quadrupeds) run faster, they use more energy. Kangaroos are different. Starting to hop uses a lot of energy, but a kangaroo uses less energy once in motion. In fact, between 4 and 16 miles (6 and 25 km) per hour they use less energy as their speed increases. Thereafter, the amount of energy they expend remains steady, up to a speed of about 25 miles (40 km) per hour.

CRUISING SPEED

The comfortable cruising speed for a red kangaroo is about 16 miles (25 km) per hour. At this speed, it makes about two hops per second, each about 12 feet (4 m) long. When it needs to go faster, it takes longer strides, until it reaches about 25 miles (40 km) per hour, a speed at which it can cruise for more than a mile. In an emergency, it can hop faster as well as longer, until it reaches a top speed of as much as 44 miles (70 km) per hour. However, it can maintain this speed for only a few hundred yards.

LEGS AND TAIL

How does a kangaroo do it? Its skeleton—especially its leg tendons—are specially adapted for this unique and very efficient way of moving. The long hind legs act as powerful levers, driven by enormously strong muscles, and the tail serves as a counter balance to prevent the kangaroo from falling on its nose as it lands. But the real secret of the kangaroo's speed is in the strong, elastic tendons in its hind legs and back.

As the kangaroo hits the ground after each leap, the tendons stretch, like giant rubber bands. This stores energy that, when released, throws the kangaroo back up into the air and forward, with hardly any more energy needed. The weight of the swinging tail adds to the effect, stretching the tendons as the kangaroo lands.

A SPRING IN ITS STEP—HOW A KANGAROO HOPS

Tendons stretch...

...and contract again

22

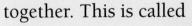

Walking on All Fives

A typical kangaroo is unable to walk. At slow speeds it uses its tail to form a tripod with its two relatively small forelimbs. It then swings its heavy hind legs forward together. This is called "crawl-walking."

Legs swing forward...   ...ready to land.

23

CHAPTER 5
Food and Feeding

The age of a kangaroo can be determined to within a year by measuring how far forward its back teeth have moved.

Sheep and goats need about twice as much food each day as an average-sized kangaroo.

In long dry seasons, when grass stops growing, red kangaroos may eat shrubs, like their ancestors once did.

Kangaroos, but not wallabies, have sharp ridges on their molars so that they can chew up tough grass.

Bacteria in the digestive tract of a kangaroo can break down poisons from some plants, making them safe to eat.

Because both animals graze on grass in a similar way, the head of kangaroos and deer are remarkably similar, although they are not related at all.

Although their distant ancestors were omnivorous or carnivorous, all modern kangaroos are herbivores, feeding mainly on grass but also on a wide variety of small plants, depending on the season and on the weather. Their teeth are specialized for this diet: the incisors at the front cut the grass off close to the ground, and the molars further back chop and grind it so that it can be swallowed. The incisors of kangaroos are rather like those of deer or sheep, adapted to eating

With a long jaw and powerful chewing muscles, a kangaroo's head is much like that of a deer.

short grass. Because the two sides of the lower jaw are not joined together, the lower incisors spread apart as the kangaroo closes its mouth, so that it can take a wider bite than a deer.

A red kangaroo can snip off grass very close to the ground with its sharp incisors.

KANGAROO TEETH

Another distinctive characteristic of kangaroo teeth is their grinding molars. Grass contains silica, a hard mineral that tends to wear down the teeth of grazing animals. Most other herbivores combat this wear by having molars that grow throughout their life, but kangaroos have evolved a different solution to the problem. As their molars wear down, they move forward and eventually fall out, to be replaced by fresh teeth that grow in the back of the jaw.

Modern kangaroos do not need as large a stomach as their browsing ancestors. However, like other herbivores, they need help in digesting the grass that they eat because they cannot break down the cellulose, of which plants are largely made. This is done by bacteria that live in the stomach of the kangaroo. The kangaroo actually lives on the portion of the food that the bacteria do not use.

DIET

Different kangaroos prefer different foods. The red kangaroo, which lives in the dry, open outback, eats mainly dry grasses, even when it has the choice of much juicier plants. This is because it needs to fill its stomach with plenty of food. Juicy grasses are very bulky, containing water that takes up too much space.

Gray kangaroos, on the other hand, can manage well on fresh, soft grasses. The reason for this is not clear, but it might be that as woodland animals not accustomed to drought like the red kangaroo, they are more prepared to "waste" water by excreting it, while the red kangaroo tends to hold it in its system.

In dry weather, all kangaroos hold their food in their digestive system for a longer time, to make sure that they digest it completely and

A red kangaroo drinking from a farmer's pond in the outback. Being adapted to desert life, kangaroos do not need to drink as often as sheep.

extract the last drop of moisture from it. Gray kangaroos have to drink three times as often as reds during the summer. They also become dehydrated much more quickly when water is scarce. This is probably because in their natural woodland habitat they do not need to conserve water in the same way as the desert-adapted red kangaroos.

When they are feeding in a group, or "mob," all kangaroos seem to take a turn to have the first bite at the grass. Those feeding at the back of the group hop or crawl around to the front when they have eaten the grass closest to them, and then stay there grazing until the others have passed them. Then they hop to the front once more.

No Competition

Large kangaroos are often accused by farmers of eating growing crops and of competing with sheep and cattle for food and water. Studies have shown that although they do damage crops—up to one–fourth of the harvest in some dry, marginal areas—there is no measurable competition between kangaroos and livestock for feed, except in times of drought, when it is the kangaroos that lose out.

I DIDN'T KNOW THAT!

CHAPTER 6
Reproduction

Everyone's favorite image of a kangaroo is a mother with a well-grown baby (known as a joey) peeping out of her pouch. Most small marsupials have hidden,

A "blue flyer" (female red kangaroo) with a well-grown joey in her pouch. The joey is nearly ready to live independently.

At birth, all baby kangaroos weigh less than about one-thirtieth of an ounce (1 gram) and are about the size of a baked bean.

Female kangaroos become sexually mature between 14 months and two years of age—later in dry seasons.

Most male kangaroos are mature at two or three years of age, except for the eastern gray, which reaches maturity at four.

Red kangaroo babies are attached to their mother's teat for the first four months of their life. They take their first look outside when they are five months old.

The smaller red kangaroo is about to lose this fight, to the stronger male on the left.

backward-facing pouches and move on all fours, but kangaroos move in an upright position and have a pouch that opens on top.

Red kangaroo females can become ready to mate at any time throughout the year. Gray kangaroos mate and give birth during the southern summer—between October and March—and antilopine kangaroos in the fall—March or April. Nearby males can tell by a scent in the female's urine that she is ready to mate. Sometimes rival males will fight over a female, with the female choosing the largest and strongest male to mate with.

GIVING BIRTH

Kangaroos usually give birth to one young; twins are very rare. The young joey is born after only 12 or 13 days' gestation. For two days before she gives birth, the mother licks out her pouch thoroughly, to make sure that it is perfectly clean. An hour or two before birth, she adopts a special birth position, leaning against a rock or a tree with her hind legs stretched out in front of her. The newborn joey is blind and hairless, but is able to move. It climbs up through the fur on its mother's belly, using special claws on its front feet, and into her pouch, where it will complete its development. Once there, it attaches itself to one of her four teats and begins to feed.

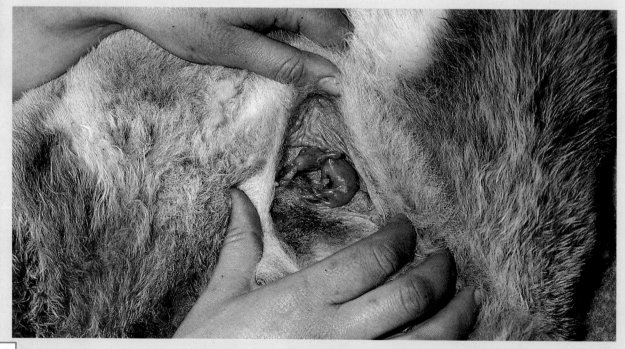

I DIDN'T KNOW THAT

The First Journey

The joey's journey from birth canal to pouch is less than two feet (60 cm) long, but it is the most important of its whole life. It starts within ten or fifteen seconds after the joey is born, and takes only three minutes to complete. This ten day-old red kangaroo joey is still smaller than the researcher's thumb.

A mother red kangaroo makes it difficult for her joey to climb back into her pouch by bending forward: it will soon be time for him to leave for the last time.

Not all fertilized eggs produce young straight away. Two or three days after she has had her first baby, a red kangaroo mother mates again, but this egg stops developing when it is only about a hundredth of an inch (a fourth of a millimeter) in diameter. It will wait, often many months before developing further, until the mother's pouch is next empty. Wallabies do the same, but eastern gray kangaroos do not. Instead of mating immediately after giving birth, they wait until the baby in the pouch is six months old.

The baby stays in the pouch for several months. Red kangaroo joeys first emerge after about six months, but other species wait even longer before coming out for the first time. The longest is the western gray, at ten months on average, varying by maybe a month either way. The joeys of other species stay in the pouch for an average of seven months.

THE JOEY

For some weeks after this, the joey returns regularly to the pouch, to rest and feed or to take shelter in case of alarm. A joey will sometimes run up to its mother at full speed and dive into her pouch headfirst, turning a somersault inside, so that its head pokes out after a few seconds of tumbling about. The joey rides in the pouch even when it is quite large, often leaning out to nibble grass while its mother grazes. Finally, though,

A gray kangaroo mother suckling her large joey. It will not be allowed to enter the pouch, because she has another small joey growing inside.

it will leave for the last time, never to return.

The time this takes also varies with the species. A red kangaroo joey returns to its mother's pouch for seven weeks on average, while gray kangaroos have this freedom only for between four and five weeks.

The longest supplier of "bed and breakfast" for baby is the antilopine kangaroo, at eight and a half weeks. While the joey is using her pouch in this way, the mother cannot rear another baby in it, because the disturbance of the joey climbing in and out would harm it. When she is ready to clean her pouch out for her next birth, the joey is no longer allowed to climb in, although it can still come to feed while it stands on the ground outside. When it does this, it uses the teat it grew up on, which by now has become very large. The new, tiny joey attaches itself to one of the other three teats, which are still very small.

A red kangaroo joey is weaned—that is, its mother no longer suckles it, and it lives entirely on grass—about a year after it is born. Grays take much longer to wean their young—about eighteen months on average.

By the time it is eight months old, the joey can keep up with its mother as she bounds across the plain.

CHAPTER 7
Social Behavior

Kangaroos running alongside cars on country roads can make leaps as long as 42 feet (13 m).

Kangaroos can jump fences as high as 10 feet (3 m) if they are being chased by dogs.

Attacking dogs are regularly killed by the kangaroo's sharp hind claws.

Kangaroos are very sociable animals that live comfortably as a group. The closest relationship between individuals is that of a mother and her offspring, which often stays with her even after it is weaned. The larger species are the more outgoing, though loosely so, moving around in groups of three to ten members. Groups are continuously changing their form; an individual may feed with one group one day and another the next. A home range will be grazed by several groups comprising about fifty kangaroos in all. This is known as a mob. The mob does not have a regular leader, but

Kangaroos like to feed in small groups, rather than alone, but they do not have a settled social system.

A young red kangaroo joey grooming his mother; this is more important as a sign of affection than a means of keeping her fur clean.

sniffing. This is a friendly gesture that conveys information about the two animals including their social standing. Sometimes the smaller of the two will crouch close to the ground, with its head quivering, to indicate submission to its new, larger acquaintance.

because the males compete for the chance to mate, the largest and strongest male in a mob is often the father of most of the offspring.

TOUCH

Kangaroos are almost completely silent, except for faint bleating sounds made by the small joeys, and soft clucking sounds made by males during courtship. Most of their communication is done by touch and body language.

When a new kangaroo comes to join a mob, it greets other members by touching noses and

GROOMING

Mothers groom their young during or just after suckling, but adults rarely groom each other. When the joey nuzzles its mother's pouch, this can be a sign that it wants to feed or perhaps that it wants to pop its head inside for a moment, only for reassurance. Mothers and young often pretend to fight, holding each other around the neck and wrestling, with the joey kicking at its mother. This is good training for adult life, especially for males who have to fight to establish their position in society.

FIGHTING

Serious fights are rare, though they sometimes occur between two equally powerful males competing for a female. These battles can be spectacular, as the two wrestle and kick, but they do not happen without warning. Kangaroos have a number of threatening gestures and acts that serve to warn other kangaroos that they are feeling aggressive.

Fights can start over quite small things, not just when males are competing for a mate. All kangaroos like to have their own space for resting in the shade, for example, and brief but rather fierce fights can arise when two males want the same lounging spot. The displays that precede these fights are obvious even to a watching human. In the first and most mild warning gesture, the kangaroo sits upright very straight and then rises to tiptoe with forearms stretched out in front. The next most serious is called "stiff-legged walking." In this threat, only the tip of the tail and the fore and hind toes touch the ground, as the male struts around his rival with his back arched.

ARM-LICKING

An unusual form of threat display is licking the forearms, which is

KANGAROO THREAT DISPLAYS

1. Kangeroos sit up very straight.

2. "Stiff-legged walking."

3. Arm-licking signals kangaroo is ready to fight.

really a way of keeping cool in hot weather. The skin here is thin and well-supplied with blood vessels, as well as being shaded from the sun. As the mixed water and saliva dries, it draws heat from the blood and cools the animal. However, when a large male does it, it is a signal that he is getting ready for a fight.

When a fight begins, it follows certain rules, which the males learn from their mothers while they are small. The two stand face to face, grappling with their forepaws, each trying to push the other backward. Their heads are thrown back, to protect their eyes and ears from being scratched. This is sometimes called "boxing," though they do not actually try to hit one another with their front paws. Until about the 1960s, it was considered highly amusing to put boxing gloves onto kangaroos so that men could pretend to box with them. The practice was very dangerous for the men, some of whom were badly injured or even killed by kicks from the frightened kangaroo.

Boxing Roos

Sometimes one kangaroo balances on his tail and kicks at the other's belly with powerful hind legs; this looks very threatening, but it is actually a sign that he thinks he is going to lose the fight and is about to give up. These kicks rarely land on target, but if they do, they can cause serious injury.

CHAPTER 8
Threats and Conservation

Most species of kangaroo and wallaby are actually increasing in numbers, as more of the outback is farmed for sheep.

Many species of smaller marsupial are endangered by loss of habitat and competition with introduced animals.

Around three million large kangaroos are shot in Australia every year.

The future for kangaroos probably lies in establishing national parks and other reserves where they can be allowed to live unharmed.

When the first European explorers ventured away from the coasts into the center of Australia in the early 19th century, they were daunted by its emptiness. They took only salt and ammunition with them, expecting to find food and water in the wilderness, as they had in other "unexplored" countries

In the United States, flocks are measured in "sheep per acre," but in Australia it is more often "acres per sheep." After good rains, these pastures look lush and green, but in dry conditions farmers resent sharing their precious grass with kangaroos.

Water is also a valuable resource. Here a thirsty gray kangaroo, with a joey to feed, drinks from a carefully filled dam.

before. But in Australia there was little to shoot or to drink. Many of them did not return.

TODAY'S LANDSCAPE

Today, the Australian environment has been changed completely by the efforts of ranchers to provide water and grazing for sheep and cattle. Although this has harmed many small animals, the large

kangaroos, especially the red, have actually benefited from the farmers' activities. For them, water stored in dams, alongside pastures cultivated for sheep, has helped create ideal living conditions. The larger species of kangaroo are far more widespread today than they were when Europeans first arrived in Australia. Indeed, they are regarded by many ranchers as pests. For more than 100 years, kangaroos have been persecuted to protect the grazing lands and water supplies established for sheep and cattle.

KANGAROO PRODUCTS

Today kangaroos are shot in large numbers for their skins and to make pet food. For years, the United States was the main market for kangaroo leather, which was used to make shoes and especially baseball gloves. Between 1973 and 1981 the import of kangaroo products was banned, because some species of kangaroo were thought to be endangered. When the status of the large species was found to be secure, the ban was lifted, and kangaroos are once again hunted. Kangaroo meat is even eaten by people in several countries besides Australia. With its low fat content, it is considered very healthy and suitable for heart patients and others needing a low-cholesterol diet.

RISING POPULATIONS

Using computer models, scientists have calculated that if between 10 and 15 percent of the population of large kangaroos were to be shot for

The long-nosed potoroo is one of the few smaller kangaroos that is still common, living in damp woods as far away from people and their dogs as possible.

commercial use every year, the population would fall to about 65 percent of what it is now. This level would be more acceptable to farmers, but the harvest would produce far more meat and skins than the market demands. So overall, the population of large kangaroos is flourishing.

ENDANGERED SPECIES

The same is not true of the smaller, less conspicuous species. Rat-kangaroos are under severe pressure in the wild, partly from competition with rabbits, which eat their food, and partly from foxes, which eat them. Neither rabbits nor foxes are native to

The rufous hare wallaby is an endangered species, surviving only in small groups in the Tanami Desert in central Australia and on two offshore islands in Western Australia.

Australia; both were introduced to the island continent since European settlement. As a result of this competition, two species of smaller kangaroos have become extinct, and three more are endangered. Small wallabies, bettongs, and bandicoots are suffering the same fate, as the woodlands where they live are cleared to grow crops and rear cattle. Potoroos, like so many of their small relations, are hunted by foxes and dogs, and they too are losing much of their habitat.

41

ROADSIDE DANGERS

Another new threat to large kangaroos comes from the increase in the number of cars on Australian roads. Kangaroos like to gather on roads in the outback at night, to lick up the dew that forms there. Because of this collection of dew, grass grows better along roads than on the open plain, which makes such spots even more attractive to hungry kangaroos.

Dangers on outback roads come in various shapes and sizes. This sign warns drivers about the risk of damaging collisions, but to kangaroo and wombat populations, cars are a very real threat.

For these reasons, there are many automobile accidents involving kangaroos. When a mother kangaroo is killed, her joey often survives the accident, though without its mother's milk it will soon die.

Raising Joey

An orphaned joey can be raised by hand, providing it is bigger than 8 inches (20 cm) long when it is found. The two most important things are to keep it warm and to provide it with the right kind of milk. An old sweatshirt with the armholes sewn shut makes a good artificial pouch, hung on the wall in a warm place so that it just touches the floor. Kangaroos cannot digest lactose (the sugar in cow's milk), so they need to be fed with treated milk in which the lactose has been converted to glucose. Some brands of canned condensed milk are suitable if they are diluted with water and have liquid vitamins added. A special formula kangaroo milk is available in Australian pet shops for this purpose.

Glossary

ABORIGINE – native Australian, the "original" people who were there when the first Europeans arrived

CARNIVORE – an animal that eats meat rather than plants

DISPLAY – behavior that shows an animal's intentions

EMBRYO – a fertilized egg before it is born

EUCALYPTUS – an Australian tree

EXTINCT – no longer existing anywhere on Earth

FOSSIL – remains or imprints of plants and animals that have become part of rocks

GENUS – a group of related species

GESTATION – the time between mating and birth

HERBIVORE – an animal that eats only plants

MARSUPIAL – an animal whose young develop in a pouch

OMNIVORE – an animal that eats both plants and animals

OUTBACK – the wide open spaces away from the settled area on the east coast of Australia

PLACENTAL – an animal whose young develop inside the mother's body

PREHENSILE – able to grasp objects

QUADRUPED – an animal that has four legs

RODENT – an animal with sharp, continuously growing front teeth, like a rat

SPECIES – a type of animal or plant

TENDON – tough, stringy material that joins muscles to bones

TUBER – the underground storage part of some plants

Further Reading

Lepthien, Emile U. *Kangaroos*. New York: Children's Press, 1995.

Meadows, Vial. *Kangaroos*. Carlsbad, CA: Dominie Press, Inc., 2000.

Swan, Erin Pembrey. *Kangaroos and Koalas: What They Have in Common*. Danbury, CT: Franklin Watts, 2000.

Woodward, John. *Kangaroos (Endangered)*. Tarrytown, NY: Benchmark, 1997.

Acknowledgments

Bruce Coleman: Cover (Staffan Widstrand); **NHPA**: page 11 (Martin Harvey), 12 (Ken Griffiths), 13 (Daniel Heuclin), 14 (Dave Watts), 15 (Martin Harvey), 18 (Daniel Heuclin), 20/21 (Martin Harvey), 23 (Daniel Zupanc), 25 (Ann & Steve Toon), 26 (A.N.T.), 27 (Ken Griffiths), 28 & 29 (Martin Harvey), 30 (A.N.T.), 31 (Patrick Fagot), 32 (Martin Harvey), 33 (A.N. T.), 34 (Martin Harvey), 35 (Patrick Fagot), 37 (Dave Watts), 38/39 (A.N.T.), 40 (Martin Harvey), 42 (Daniel Zupanc); **Oxford Scientific Films**: page 9 (Belinda Wright), 10 (Kathie Atkinson), 16 (Kenneth Day), 17 (Jen & Des Bartlett), 19 (Belinda Wright), 24 (Steve Turner), 39 (Jen & Des Bartlett),40 (Rudie H Kuiter), 43 (Kathie Atkinson); All background images © Steck-Vaughn Collection (Corbis Royalty Free, Getty Royalty Free, and StockBYTE)..

Index

Numbers in *italic* indicate pictures